Slow Down, Show up & live

INTRODUCTION

This book is based on what I have found to be the three fundamental truths I have found that consistently underpin every decent and impactful theory I have found in the world of psychotherapy, Neuroscience, neurolinguistic programming and coaching.

I have whittled it all down to what I believe are the essentials in creating a life and a version of the self that you can enjoy, love and create every single day.

It requires commitment and responsibility but it is a lot of fun and has infinite possibilities.

If you take away all of the noise and opinion out of your world then I believe to be happy all you need to do is simple:

Find space to see where you are in life and what is actually around you, decide on who you want to be and then live life fully and from the heart.

This book is written for you.

Please read it as such, play full out and be committed and you can change the world.

Slow down, show up and live.

Cheers
Phil

For Caroline, Fred, Ells and George

If home is where the heart is, then you are all always my home.

I love you

CONTENTS

1. The Candle in the Kiln
2. Coaching
3. Why you're here
4. The creation of what is possible
5. Possibility and office refurbishment
6. Creating change
7. Commitment
8. The three truths of a happy life
9. Too easy?
10. WARNING
11. SLOWING DOWN
12. The practice of going slow
13. Self-exploration
14. Happiness is…
15. You have arrived
16. SHOW UP
17. The model for change
18. The EGO
19. Questions to help you show up
20. Creation
21. Commitment to BEING
22. You speak your world
23. Matthew's story
24. Take responsibility
25. LIVE
26. Self-forgiveness
27. Self-forgiveness - A reflection
28. Not feeling good enough
29. Confidence
30. Fighting what 'is'
31. Relationships
32. Relationships Truth

33. The myth of the 50/50 relationship
34. Self-love
35. Authentic VS Conditioned Self
36. Self-love VS Self-care
37. Closing thoughts
38. A page of gratitude

THE CANDLE IN THE KILN

I have always loved the human mind and self-improvement. When I was younger it boarded on addiction, I had a firm belief that my friendship group would be my group forever because when we got drunk we talked about the deep stuff (in actual practice it was drunk guys repeating with emphasis the phrase "But what is it FOR" in various ways).

I used to believe that my deep thinking on everything meant I was different from everyone, I was an overthinker, I genuinely used to give real thought when staff at a clothing shop would ask if I wanted the receipt in the bag or emailed to me.

If I was at an airport I would be morally obliged to buy ANY book on self-help, thoughtful reflection or anything that would make me a nightmare to travel with.

If you were trying to enjoy the sun and a giant bearded man kept prodding you and asking you to contemplate reality and the self you may start to understand my wife's struggle.

I think this is why when I worked in the banking industry for 17 years I felt empty, my level of deep thought hit a ceiling very quickly, and mortgage rates are not really 'it' for me. So I eventually had an inner collapse on an epic scale.

I was exhausted beyond belief, my first son Fred had been born and I'm pretty sure didn't sleep for around 2 years, I was working 5-6 days a week full time, and I had decided to start my studies as a psychotherapist on a night until after 10 pm, I worked free weekend days for free doing therapy hours in an NHS clinic, I studied, I travelled two hours back and forth to Newcastle for band practice, I tried to exercise and be in a shape that wasn't just "potato" and within all of this, I wanted to be a husband and father.

It tired me out just writing that. I wasn't burning the candle at both ends I was putting it in a kiln.

I wanted to show up fully for everyone and thus barely showed up for anyone, including myself.

Sitting on my sofa at 3 am, listening to music the ceiling started to slowly meltdown on me, small droplets at first then big ones, like I was having paint ooze down onto me, I curled up in a ball and had my first breakdown hallucination.

I needed to make a change.

COACHING

I used to hold the same thoughts on life coaching that most British people do, either; "A person who is just a cheerleader and uses the noise 'whoop' too much" OR "Why on earth would I need someone to just tell me how to live my life?" (Neither are true)

However, after years of therapy, I was still at square one. In my experience of therapy, I like to use this metaphor.

I am trapped in a burning house, therapy will tell me everything I need to know about the fire, the temperature it burns, how it interacts in each room, each material, the long history of fire and what it means to me.

This is all great, but for me, it never told me the most important thing:

HOW TO PUT OUT THE FIRE!!

My friend Jane, at a barbeque at our other friend's house in London, had suggested in a drunken stupor that I try out a podcast by a man called Jay Shetty. It sounded good, I loved deep thought, so I listened, I loved, and I still do. If you don't then I recommend it.

So after a really awful meeting with a therapist provided by my university, I decided to look into his stuff, which led me to explore the world of coaching.

I stroked my beard for effect and saw there was a discount on a coaching course.

My knowledge of what coaching is was nothing.

I googled coaches near me, I was curious.

A wonderful woman called Jude Daunt appeared on my Google machine and I contacted her and we booked our session.

It was deep, it was heartfelt, it was emotional, but it was light and hopeful. What was this sorcery? I booked more sessions, I signed up for Jay's course. I needed to dive into this world.

Jude later referred me on to my current coach, mate and all-around top bloke David Wilkinson who picked up the ball and ran with it.

I had not only started to learn how to put the fire out, but the possibility of rebuilding, repairing and making an even better house was starting to emerge.

That is the beauty of a coaching approach.

WHY YOU'RE HERE

Right enough about me, this book is about you!

I just wanted to set a context for you as to where I am coming from.

I am not a monk, like Jay, I am not a world-famous coach like Tony Robbins, I am not Gandhi bringing about world change on a political level (yet)

But I don't have to be, they all have beautiful words and thoughts of deep wisdom.

However, I am a regular person, who was in such deep traumatic inner pain struggling to live an ordinary everyday life in an underprivileged forgotten city in the northeast of England called Sunderland.

A person who has struggled with relationships, money, parenthood, career, purpose, friendships, morality and love.

I am someone who felt so deeply empty like a huge piece was always missing in himself and couldn't enjoy success and love so much that I wanted to end my life many times.

Now I am a person who has found out how to love every day, create business and financial success, have my heart grow and be filled every day through love, connect with others and live purposefully and authentically.

This book is taking the years and countless hours of experience, research and experimenting I have gone through to get there and show you the three fundamental truths of how to enjoy life from the heart and love who you are.

That is what we all want right? It is why we want money and things, it is why we want to look good it is why we want to do well in academia?

Because we believe achieving these things will bring us satisfaction and make us worthy of love.

You can convince yourself it is about something else if you want, but if you break it down that is the root. It is the truth we are all born with and we all lose at some point.

Everybody wants to be happy.

Everybody wants to be loved.

THE CREATION OF WHAT IS POSSIBLE

Throughout this book, I have included exercises and thought pieces which will be in bold and italicised. With each one, I would like you to consider, put the book down and give yourself ten minutes or more to ponder the answer.

I designed this book so you can do this in small chunks. Read an idea, insight or thought then go for a walk, have a bath, get a cuppa or whatever clears space for your mind to think about the questions or activities presented.

I promise you, if you give these some real-time, thought and care you will get tremendous value from this book.

If you want to create change with me I need you to commit to playing full out. No half measures.

Each piece is not designed to be swallowed, accepted or even totally understood on first reading.

Rather each one looks to create 'Possibility'.

If we can accept that some of these things would be possible then we have created a new choice in our ways to be and from that, we can powerfully choose to create change or we can stay on the path we are on.

But either way, you get to CHOOSE, you get to act from a position of control in your life.

In possibility and creation lies really powerful transformation.

POSSIBILITY AND OFFICE REFURBISHMENT

I want you to imagine a small 3-person office, empty and plain.

We discuss the things that you can do in that office, maybe get three desks and computers in there, maybe 2 desks and a sofa, we could get a small group in for a meeting, we could host a small party maybe but it would be cramped.

Now, what if I ask you to imagine a big birthday party, or a gig or a parade.

Your mind can not fathom how that would work, because it is constrained by its limitation of what happens in that space.

When we always turn up with the same thoughts, actions and beliefs we have always had, we put these small office walls on the results we can achieve. Our results can only be so big because our minds can not imagine or accept that there are other ways for it to be.

If you feel stuck then I want you to know you created that stuckness in your mind.

If you feel like you get the same results and never progress I invite you to consider there are ways to move the office walls out, WAY out.

If you can consider the possibility that you have created your way of BEING in the world in your mind then you have to also accept the possibility that you can rewire and create a new and better way.

It's time for an office refurbish.

CREATING CHANGE

I am making an assumption that firstly, you reading this are beautiful (nailed that one) and secondly, you are someone looking to change something in your life. Whether that is relationship, job, success or just how you relate to yourself.

One of the most powerful and undeniable lessons I have learned on my journey is that real change CAN NOT happen outside of yourself.

No matter how much you want to, you can never change what someone else thinks, feels or does. You do not have that power. As much as you want to. Imagine if I came into your world and started telling you how to be, you would hopefully tell me where to go.
The same is true in life.

If we want to create real change in our worlds then that has to come from within. It comes from the inner work and that is what the questions and insights in this book are designed to start. Think of it as dipping your toe into the pool of inner work.

By doing this we can change how we show up in the world and both myself and my clients have all reported a seemingly universal phenomenon, the world just seems to shift around you. Just by you being different, people are now treating you differently, opportunities seem to appear out of thin air, and broken relationships heal.

It is not a miracle, there is good old science behind it which I will explain in this book.

But I want you to know that underpinning all of this work is YOU.

The change in your world happens inside out.

COMMITMENT

We are all only as good as our word.

There is little power in try, there is little power in want.

There is a universe moving power in making a commitment.

THAT is what I am asking of you today.

Not a commitment to me or anyone else, but rather a personal inner commitment to show up to the ideas presented in this book and play full out.

A commitment to showing up as your best self.

A commitment to showing up to everything in life with authentic energy and live life from the heart.

Write it down, speak it out, hang it on the wall, whatever you do commit for you.

THE THREE TRUTHS OF A HAPPY LIFE

Ok, so from the jump I want to tell you, that I HATE gimmicky things, especially in coaching. I hate the "five ways to beat anxiety forever and live like a flower" or "Supercharge your inner awesome to get all the money yeah!" (I hate them so much I just found out I am horrible at making them up)

As someone who has spent thousands of pounds and hours on books, courses, meetings, seminars and everything in-between, I know it can be tough to not buy into the gimmicks. If someone happens to hit the right pain point for you then you are hooked. I know this from working with a marketing company that kept showing me how to hit pain points, it was gross.

After undergoing all of this and reflecting on it I believe that everyone is pretty much telling you the same things. They take a well-trodden path, slap their personality and gimmick on it and there you go, new content. As Alan Partridge would say "they just rebadged it you fool"

My intention for this book is to strip all of the noise away, save you countless hours and money and show you what in my experience works.

This is from the countless hours of therapy, psychotherapy, NLP and coaching I have done for clients and myself.

I believe (because I have seen it, taught it and lived through it) that if you just stick to these three things every day you can live a life of enjoyment, love and success.

Exciting right?

It should be.

TOO EASY?

As the queen of pop-punk Avril Lavigne once said "why'd you have to go and make things so complicated?" to which I answer, I didn't Avril and I am starting to think this song isn't even about me.

One of the hardest lessons I ever had to learn for myself is that "things don't always have to be hard"

Where I am from, graft and grit are high-value traits.

You suffer to get the pize. Does anything hold value or weight without suffering or turmoil?

When my coach David told me that not everything has to be a difficult struggle I felt something pull in me like I had been jolted to a stop.

What was he even talking about? Is that possible? Is that a way that someone can be?

I spent a long time reflecting on this phrase, it was powerful for me.

I offer that to you now, you do not have to struggle to get to the prize.

There is not some arduous journey where at the end of this book you will be radically changed.

You are right where you need to be, right now. There is no future improved version of you, there is only ever you right now at this moment. You just have to 'BE' (more on that later)

But that is pretty simple, right? You are doing it right now.

Keep doing it as we move on and I promise you, that you are making the right amount of progress at every stage. It is that EASY!

Great, so let's look at these truths, shall we?

WARNING

Ok so I am going to be honest and authentic with you here (You will see it is the only way to be)

This book drives deep into who you are and as such it will hit subjects that a lot of people are uncomfortable with.

I know that especially being raised in a boat-building city in the North East of England, subjects like 'self-love' and 'inner being' were not ever really up for discussion.

Men especially struggle with the subject of love for the self because a lot of us were raised to fight it or stay away from it. Women I find want to talk about it but struggle more with allowing it for themselves.

Whatever your aversions might be, I want you to know, that in order to get different results, we need to try different methods. You can love yourself without screaming it from the rooftops while wearing a heart locket with two pictures of yourself in it.

The absolute foundation of a happy life is love, respect and full value of the self.

No one loves me as much as I do and I say that not with arrogance, but with complete compassion and respect.

Learn to fully love and accept who you are and the world feels so much lighter.

Once you master that, you've won the game.

Let go of your preconceptions and approach this fully open-minded, we are creating new possibilities with new thinking.

"Everybody in the world is seeking happiness - and there is one sure way to find it. That is by controlling your thoughts.

Happiness doesn't depend on outward conditions. It depends on your inner conditions"

-From 'how to win friends and influence people'

THE FIRST TRUTH
SLOWING DOWN

More than any other piece of wisdom I could share, this one is the foundation for everyone and can sometimes be the toughest one to grasp.

We live in a world that just forces 'doing' on us constantly.

I bet while you are reading this you could create an 'I should be doing XYZ" phrase.

So many people I have worked with have felt like they do not 'have time'. They have to work all day and night, then all the little jobs in between. They are always on the go, they are just doing and doing. They eventually burn out and the ceiling starts melting down onto them!

If this rings true for you, I ask you you this powerful question and want you to think about it:

What are you working for?

Think about that, take 20 minutes and come back, I will pause the book.

Hey, welcome back!

Most people work themselves to the bone so they can have holidays so that they can enjoy a break from…..work?

The truth is our world tells us our value often lies in work, if someone asks what we 'do' we tell them our profession and they pretend to care.

Is that what we 'do'? Is that our function? Our output in life? Have we become that linked to our work.

Ask me what I do and you will hear "well I love my kids, I go on adventures, I connect with people on a level deeper than you could imagine, I learn, I love my wife with a passion, I create a world of magnificence". People never forget what I 'do'.

So if you are working to create a life of enjoyment and love and yet you are up all night, stressed and miserable but thinking "one day at the end of all of this I will be happy" then I have some awful news for you.

In this initial section of the book, I invite you to engage in the practice of slowing down.

The single most valuable phrase I have ever heard has been the following:

SLOW DOWN, TO SPEED UP

The creator of the world's fastest car was talking about driving it and said "If you want to go fast, you have to go smooth, if you want to go smooth you have to go slow"

If you put your foot down on the pedal, you can not navigate unforeseen weather or tight corners and the engine will damage and burn out.

However, if you can learn and practice slowing down these things become easier to navigate and while the pedal-to-the-floor types are struggling to turn you can navigate with an ease that puts you out in front.

I am not a car guy, but this has always made sense to me.

If we are always going so fast in life then we can navigate the unforeseen or upcoming things and will be frustrated and slowed down by them.

THE PRACTICE OF GOING SLOW

I am not suggesting that you live life like a turtle that has become a monk.

A lot of people are shocked when I say this but life is there to be enjoyed and lived, juice that lemon! (I just came up with that phrase off the cuff and although I am leaving it in, I am appalled by it)

However what I am suggesting is that we all need, as humans, an ability to slow down and connect with ourselves every day.

This can look like many different things for many different people.

Personally, I take 10 minutes at the start of my day to close my eyes, breathe deeply and listen to a meditation track on Spotify (I will list it at the end of the book if you want to check it out). I also always commit to 30+ minutes of exercise per day.

That is it for me, I box breathe when I need to slow down so 4 seconds in, hold for 4, out for 4 and hold for 4.

Find your slowdown starter, it can be getting a hot or cold drink and focusing on the temperature, smell, colour, cup, taste and every detail of it that brings you into the present. It may be reading or walking in nature. Only you know what works for you.

It sets me up. When I can feel my thoughts getting built up, negative or I feel overwhelmed I engage with slowing down, looking at the present moment and what can I do in it?

We are so often in this self-created rush to do things and be something and by doing this we create this idea that our happiness is just around the corner in the future.

Can you tell me what it is like to live in the future?
No, because no one can, because you only ever live in this moment now.
Everything in the future is created and held in your mind.

I want you to consider that by putting your happiness in the future, you are telling your mind it is not available for you now and since we are only ever living in the now, happiness becomes an incredibly difficult thing to attain regularly.

We can become like the donkey walking toward the carrot on the stick, believing if we keep walking we will be closer to the carrot but it is always out in front of us in a place we aren't.

SELF EXPLORATION

So why do we slow down? What is the purpose of us going slow?

We are all so busy getting somewhere else that we forget to see where we are standing right now.

Sometimes there is a need to slow down and acknowledge where you are now is ok and that you are good enough and safe.

I used to get haunted by the constant need to buy things, I spent my first year of coaching convinced I needed to be growing and offering all of these things no one else was, this lead me to be broke with an empty practice and wondering what had just happened.

My coach slowed me down into a place of seeing where I was and that it was ok, I was safe. From there I could focus on just serving each person in front of me powerfully and from there, word spread and my practice grew, then it was full, and then I had to create a waiting list.

All of my success came first and foremost by learning to slow down, accept and acknowledge where I am. Accepting what IS can be a powerful breakthrough for anyone in its own right.

Other times when negative thoughts or struggles come up slowing down allows you to truth test them. (this is asking 'is that thought factually true in the real world or something I have created in my head)

A good example of this is last night I was working with a woman in London who was concerned she was too boring. No one found her interesting and when her friends talked in-depth about politics she had nothing to say.

I asked her if she wanted to learn more about politics?

She said "No, not really, I find the subject incredibly boring"

I then asked had anyone outside of herself ever called her boring? If I was to ask any of her friends and family to describe her would boring be on anyone's list?

"No, I don't think anyone has ever said that" she replied.

When she was going at a frantic pace, this stray thought had become a punishing truth for her, when she slowed down, however, she saw this was just a belief she had created.

Slowing down in either example is examining the context we are viewing life.

We are so quick to accept the thought as hard facts and never challenge them.

Consider the possibility that despite what the world has told you and that you have possibly told yourself, you do not need to be somewhere else right now. You are exactly where you need to be and you are exactly who you need to be happy.

There is no grand race, there is no journey, you are here and that is ok.

Happiness is here for you right now.

Often this clashes with our daily perception of self, how can happiness be here right now if I am miserable?

I am not ever telling you to be anyway, I am not telling you to believe something you are not, but it is through creation and possibility that we can start to explore new ways of BEING. If you can slow down to consider this way as a possibility and accept that this exists for you as a possibility, then you now have a choice. Your power is always in making or not making that choice.

If you can consider the possibility that happiness is in you right now waiting to be tapped into, then you can start to explore what might look like.

If you always work a certain way to work, then you discover a previously hidden path, you can't unsee it. The new path means now you are making a choice every day about which one to take.

You have walked the one path all of your working life and you may think it is the safer path, it is the only one you can pick but that is a lie we tell ourselves.

You are making the choice. Make it boldly.

HAPPINESS IS…….

"Happiness is not a place to get to, it is a place to come from"

It is not out in the future, the future only exists in your mind outside the present.

Look at finding things that make you happy right now.

Take that joy to people, connect and listen to others.

When I was younger I would try and fill this unexamined inner void with drink, drugs, liaisons with women (I believe that is the polite term), lies, eating, extreme sports, joining the circus, stand-up comedy, acting out, self-harm, fighting others and worst of all getting long swooshy hair that I dyed black with a big blonde stripe in it.

I was a mess, I was lost, and I was a bad person. I am sorry to everyone if I hurt you, I was honestly doing the best with the tools I had and the self-awareness I lacked.

I worked in the UK finance industry for 17 years, I tried to quit after 1 week.

I hated it, but I stuck at it because hard work and misery are what are prescribed where I am from.

I worked hard, I got promotion after promotion, I worked with millionaires on yachts, I got my own office, I got to work in a suit every day, I bought a house in Oxford, I married my beautiful wife, we got a stinky but lovable cat.

I was so deeply miserable, that the sadness would not leave me.

The mistake I had made that we ALL make at some point, is believing that happiness, peace and life we are looking for exist out there.

I used to think " I will be happy when…..I get the promotion/house/body I want etc"

All this is telling my brain is that "Happiness is out there, in the future" and the sad part of that is the future never arrives and it never will.

The future is a construct in our mind, it is all just thought and all we EVER have is right now this moment.

So my message was always 'happiness is not here today and is a place to get to someday"

Well, how about today?

YOU HAVE ARRIVED

I want you to consider that you do not have to be in a hurry to get anywhere different in life.

Consider that there is no other place to be at all.

Nothing else to get to.

Only you existing right now in the current moment.

There will only ever be you in this current moment.

There is no future version of you that is complete, better or happier.

Only you in the here and now fully BEING all that you can be and living into your life.

How do you want to live life right now? What will be your way of BEING?

How will you show up?

What actions will you take right now?

"I AM NOT WHAT HAPPENED TO ME.

I AM WHAT I CHOOSE TO BECOME"

- Carl Jung

THE SECOND TRUTH -
SHOW UP

How we show up or our BEING is everything.

How you present your way to the world determines how the world treats you, the stories you will tell yourself from that, the beliefs you create from that and all of that combined is what creates your world.

The concept of showing up was brought to me by my coach, I thought he was bonkers.

I mean I got it on an understanding of the words he was saying level but I didn't get it.

I then started reading the works of coaches like Brene Brown, Steve Chandler, and Rich Litvin and that led me to the big boss Steve Hardison. Steve spoke in a way that connected all of the dots in my brain. He made everything the other amazing minds said that was confusing seem clear.

(I have never had the privilege of speaking with Steve and not that he needs it from me but check out his TBOLITNFL video on youtube, then buy the ultimate coach book, life-changing)

So I shall explain showing up/BEING and why it is crucial to how your world is created and how to BE a new way in the world.

THE MODEL FOR CHANGE

So if you are reading this book, I would guess there is something in life that you are looking to change.

We all are at some point.

The most common way people go about change is the one below.

1. Change the goal
2. Change the habits
3. Change the person

This nearly always fails and when we break it down it is so simple to see why as we set ourselves up to fail from the first step.

I want you to imagine a smoker going through this process.

1. Change the goal - I am a smoker and I have decided I am going to stop smoking
2. Change the Habits - I usually smoke when I drink so I will stop drinking
3. Change the person - Once I have done this long enough I will have given up smoking

The reason this method rarely works is that it is backwards. Look at the first message, " I am a smoker". The person is telling themselves that they ARE a smoker, smoking isn't something they do it is something they are. They are closing the door to possibility because the underlying message is "I am a smoker trying to be a non-smoker"

The way I work is to address this in reverse.

1. Change the person - You make a commitment to a new way of showing up, you are no longer a smoker, you are someone who simply doesn't smoke. There is no goal change, there is no habit change, you focus every day on your BEING and your commitment and BEING says that you are someone who doesn't smoke.

This is not a smoker pretending that they will become a non-smoker, this is someone who has created a new way of BEING, someone committed to showing up as themselves and that is a person who doesn't smoke.

Then the habits change naturally without thought.

You make decisions from a new way of BEING. You make decisions as a person who doesn't smoke.

The goal is reached naturally from this.

This is not a do and you will get 100% of the results you want 100% of the time.

But if you can commit to showing up in each moment from this new place, then you give yourself the best possible chance of succeeding.

I would advise you to read the section on creating new ways of showing up and revisiting this chapter.

THE EGO

In Psychology the Ego wants one thing more than all others, it wants to be right. If it is right then the world is safe and makes sense.

Even if the thing the Ego wants to be right about is harmful, it doesn't matter it only exists if it is always right.

It is why yo-yo dieting often happens, the message has been told to the Ego all its life, possibly since we were very young, that we are a fat person. The Ego identifies as this thing, it starts to highlight to you all the instances in life this is true (the time you ordered a cake, the time you binge ate etc) and it will recoil or ignore all the things that would make it wrong (the time you felt good in the mirror or the time your friend said you looked like you had lost weight).

The Ego starts showing you and building a world to fit the narrative it has been fed. The negative beliefs we often adopt in childhood, often to keep ourselves safe and feel like we fit in.

It is all a matter of safety.

If in this example you were to explore getting healthy and made progress, then your brain kicks in.

It knows that being overweight and miserable keeps you alive, it is comfortable with what life looks like in that world. If you start getting healthy then there are so many unknowns, is it safe? Is it deadly? Will we be abandoned? I know we are not abandoned when we are overweight! Let's stick to what we know is safe.

When I struggled with weight issues, nothing set me back from progress faster than someone telling me I looked good.

IS THIS COMPLICATED?

No, it is the easiest thing in the world, you are doing it right now.

BEING is just the way we are presenting and interacting with the world.

BEING is something we get to create every day.

What we are looking to do is create an awareness of the BEING we are choosing to create.

This whole book is about considering new possibilities for ways of showing up.

QUESTIONS TO HELP YOU SHOW UP

Here are a few powerful questions to answer and think about for you.

(And don't do that thing I used to do where I got a book with exercise suggestions in and I would skip those bits, get to the end of the book and wonder why the book had no real effect. Take ownership, do the work, you are worth it, my friend)

Who would I need to BE to be truly successful?

Who would I need to BE to create a life of true happiness?

Who would I need to BE to be an incredible partner?

Who would I need to BE to be surrounded by love?

Who would I need to BE to create a deep love for myself?

Who would I need to BE to create a level of confidence that is amazing?

These are questions I love to use with my clients, when we know who we need to be to get what we want then we create a blueprint or a map to the destination.

Ask yourself these questions and be honest.

Then figure out how to BE that person.

For me, when I thought about being successful I thought oh I need to make X amount as a coach, so I thought how does that guy show up each day? He works on himself, he learns and listens, he shows up for his clients and loved ones fully as himself, he creates tiny miracles when his clients get in the room, he focuses on health and sleep, he loves talking with people etc etc. Then from there I looked at how to get more of this into my life and started being that guy.

Oh, and he also wrote a kickass book.

CREATION

I want you to consider the following:

We get to create ourselves, all day, every day.

Your personality as you know it is a lie.

Well, the fixed nature of it is certainly a lie.
We start to build our personalities at a young age psychologically. Around our early teens.

We use a combination of the message our parents and others give us and what we have learned keeps us safe.

Safety doesn't always mean in a physical sense, but these can be traits that make us fit in with peer groups or keep people at arms length. These can be things such as "I am unemotional" "I am strict with time" and "I am not very confident" to name a few.

Once we take these messages on board we start to look for all the ways to prove they are true because they reinforce our belonging and safety in the world.

The mind finds them everywhere. Have you ever bought a new model of car and all of sudden you see that same make, model and colour everywhere? It isn't because they released a lot of the same but rather it is in your consciousness and your mind is picking them out now. Same with this.

So by the time we are in adulthood, we have spent years of this I AM message getting drilled into us.

Now let's consider this possibility:

If your personality is created through stories, beliefs and meaning we attach to events then our personality is entirely created and held within our minds.

Therefore can you consider the possibility that your mind can create new personalities and new ways of showing up in the world?

I understand it can be quite jarring and a tough one to accept, after all, I am challenging the very nature of you.

However, as with any part of this book, I just want you to consider the possibility of it being available. You don't have to walk the path, but just become aware the path exists.

COMMITMENT TO BEING

Something I learned from the great Steve Hardison was a commitment to our BEING.

All of my clients, when the time is right, will sit and create a way of BEING to support the life they want to live.

We write bold I AM statements and hang every single one, framed on the wall. So that when they come into my office to create magic, they know who they are showing up as and who I am showing up as.

I know some hang them up at home too, have them as a phone screen saver, and speak them to their partner or others, one guy made a poster at his place of work, I recorded mine on a voice note app and listen to it when needed during the day.

It can feel like a huge weight is lifted when we know how we are going to show up that day.

There are no exceptions for my clients and me, we are our manifesto and our manifestos are us.

I will show up from my document the same way to a checkout girl as I would the queen.

That is powerful

YOU SPEAK YOUR WORLD

The language we use is incredibly important.

It literally creates our world.

Both our inner and outer language.

If you ask any of my clients I would imagine eyes would roll as they tell you how much I am a crusty old dean for language! But it is vital.

When we speak thoughts into existence the world and ourselves react to that.

If I speak to the world that I am a shy person enough, then people will start treating me like one, I will react like one, I will make the decisions as one, I will dress, think and feel like one and all of a sudden the world shifts to accommodate and POOF I am a shy person.

We rarely stop to think of the language we are using, but often it comes from stories, beliefs and meanings that we attach to events. It creates the lens through which we all see our world.

Notice the language you are using internally and externally every day to reinforce beliefs and ideas that are not serving you, how could you change this?

MATTHEWS STORY

Matthew was a young man I worked with, incredibly bright and insightful, always willing to learn. He works as an emergency responder with the ambulance service here in the UK.

This already created a huge admiration I had for him as a man.

However, he was having difficulty with higher-ups not believing he was ready to lead and to do tasks. He was too nervous to volunteer at training events. His confidence was on life support (Medical joke of the day)

We discussed his language around these events, he was telling himself all day he wasn't ready, he went up to the decision-makers before and told them "I am not sure I am ready, I might need a bit of help, I am not a confident person" then when they got someone in to help in difficult bits he was offended.

He couldn't see he was creating his world through his language.

He was telling himself and others he lacked confidence, so he started making decisions based on this belief, which made people see him with this label, which reinforced the belief and this all happens enough that he finds himself living the life of a not confident person and wondering why people treat him this way.

Look at the language you use, look at the world your words are creating.

What would you like to create with your language?

TAKE RESPONSIBILITY

No one else is responsible for your happiness.

If this is new to you then this is the moment you need to take FULL responsibility.

A lot of us let life happen to us, we become stuck in the Victim mindset.

We put our value outside of ourselves. We let the world happen to us. We use phrases such as "they made me feel sad" or "They made me (fill in the blank)"

No one can make us feel anything we do not want to unless we decide to feel that way.

If your feelings are dependent on the actions, thoughts and words of others (which as previously mentioned we have no control over) then you are turning up in the world waiting for someone else to tell you that you are worthy of love, time or value.

All it takes is for someone to wake up on the wrong side of the bed and your value is destroyed, your worth is gone.

Your self-worth is being constantly placed on the roulette table and you are gambling each time that hopefully, your number comes up.

I want you to consider there is a healthier, more powerful way to be.

Being an Owner of life, taking that responsibility for how you react.

Understanding that your value never goes up or down in relation to what others do or say, what job you do or do not have and any other possible angle. It stays the same.

You as a person, are wholly and deeply worthy. You are worthy of love and respect and hold tremendous value just by being you.

You get to choose as an owner how something will make you feel, how you will respond and what you will make it mean as you move forward in life.

Will the horrible things your parents did mean that you are forever held back? That you are fixed into being unable to be happy? Or will you make it a valuable lesson of how you do not want to be in life, something that made you value happiness and the happiness of others?

You get to choose.

"EVERYTHING WE HEAR IS AN OPINION. NOT A FACT.

EVERYTHING WE SEE IS A PERSPECTIVE, NOT THE TRUTH"

- MARCUS AURELIUS

THE THIRD TRUTH -
LIVE

So we have looked at slowing down and seeing where we are in the world right now, we then looked at who we are showing up as in the world. This last part is the fun part (hey stop screaming at me I know it has all been fun) but living is it, it is the point, it is everything.

The purpose of the first two truths is that they allow you to shape yourself and the world that you are living in. The following chapters are all about actually living that life. These are some of the most valuable teachings I have ever created or witnessed.

I want to stress, that these rarely work without doing the deep inner work outlined in the first two truths. I designed this book specifically this way.

This is another layer deeper into you, most people never explore here and I want to acknowledge you for choosing to do so. Often this can be a breakthrough for people in itself, choosing to value yourself so much that you do the work, often this is more valuable than people have offered themselves in a long time.

SELF-FORGIVENESS

I don't know if I will have ever told you much about this, but I was raised going to church A LOT. I had no real concept of what it was all about as I was so young, I remember volunteering to play bass in the church band during my 'punk' phase and trying to jump and rock out to Christian songs was not easy and quite frankly it looked so odd.

It created this message inside me that I was life's black sheep, I was never meant to fit in. I mean if I couldn't fit into a place built on the idea of loving everyone what chance did I have?

It felt like everyone empathised with my parents for having me and judged everything I did.

I remember wanting to go to this camp I attended every year, I had made some of my closest friends there but you needed approval from the local vicar.

It was a new guy, he had just moved there to replace the old one who I was quite fond of, but this new guy didn't like me from the get-go.

I went and had a cup of tea at his house and talked about life and religion and he said to me "I am sorry Phil, I can not in good faith let you attend this camp because I believe in my heart your life is destined to lead you into hell" I was hurt, angry and all I could muster was a very British "right ok thanks then"

It was devastating, I know I had strayed into trying drink and drugs at a young age but I wasn't a dealer or addicted I was just being honest. I was aware that I liked to flirt with girls but most of the time I just really liked talking to them and hanging out. I was lonely. Now I was rejected by the house of love and acceptance.

Growing up I am not sure I processed this or understood it. To be brutally honest, some of this is just hitting me now. This message given to me by people I loved and trusted in an area like my spirituality was now rejecting me as 'bad' but I felt like a good, kind and caring person.

This haunted me as I grew, a lie that a lazy uncaring Vicar made not only became my truth but one cemented at my core.

My mind would never let me feel a part of anything, not really and anything I did was inherently wrong. I remember telling my therapist "I don't know what is eating away at me, but it is this never-ending feeling of 'wrongness'.

My journey to self-forgiveness for everything started when talking with my coach. We were talking about my life and I mentioned in quick passing my music as a silly hobby, he asked more about it and I could feel my shame flooding over me.

I always felt uncomfortable talking about it, I was objectively not good, I was told I would never do anything in music and it was at the core of me that was deemed bad.

We talked for hours about me taking ownership and responsibility for the actual things I had done that I was not proud of (they happened, I played my part, I am a better man now) but also to recognise I was carrying this baggage for someone else, it wasn't mine. I had just picked it up.

Consider your own self-forgiveness,

1 - Choose to take full and I mean FULL ownership of what you have done in life. It is yours and no one else's. Everyone is always doing their best with their mental state and life skills at the time. Me breaking up with a girl because she got her hair cut super short as a surprise when I was a kid was just an emotionally immature child not understanding change. I didn't have the tools I do now.

2- Recognise the messages, lies and stories that you have been carrying for other people. It is like you walked into a hotel, picked up someone else's heavy case and decided it is part of you now. It isn't, you can put it down now. To do this fully I would recommend working with a coach or therapist to root these things out.

SELF FORGIVENESS REFLECTION

Consider where you are feeling pain or self-doubt in your life right now. Where did the belief or view that caused this stem from? Was this actually your reality or have you been carrying someone else's baggage? (their view, opinion or belief about your/ your world)

Is it true? Can you prove it to be true?

What is the value in you holding on to this thought? Is that a healthy and productive reason to hold on to it?

Once you examine each thought with this, you create awareness and with that, you have the power to choose to let it go, set down the baggage and feel lighter.

Not feeling good enough

What even is perfection? Do you know?

What is good enough?

I am seriously asking you to consider this question right now.

So many of my clients tell me they feel like they are not good enough and I ask them all these questions.

Do you know how many I have met who have an answer? Zero.

What does a perfect/good enough parent look like?

What does the perfect/good enough version of your body look like?

What does the perfect/good enough look like?

Ask yourself now the version of the question that applies to you, because often we are beating ourselves up for not reaching a goal when we have no idea where the endpoint of the goal is.

It is like going out of your front door to run a race, except you don't know where the end goal is, and neither does anyone else, but you believe you should be there. It is madness.

Each one of us is good enough, right now, as we are.

CONFIDENCE

I had just decided to start doing stand-up comedy. Why did I do that?

I knew I loved being on stage in a band and performing, I even performed in a child version of Grease the musical (Knicky in case you wondered) BUT I also knew I hated being solo on stage, so why am I doing the most vulnerable solo thing I can think of.

Confidence was non-existent, but I had just started dating this new lady and she was so out of my league that I thought I can't just hide in the toilet now.

I was third on the bill, the first act, a young guy with floppy hair looking like a mix between Rick Moranis and John Lennon (use google) took to the stage and was so nervous he was viciously booed off. I didn't even know that happened, the poor kid looked destroyed and my nerves were at an exploding level.

The next lady took to the stage, ok time to breathe and get the crowd back, she started talking, kind of weird she was slurring a little, looked almost a bit spaced out, certainly sweating…wait…becoming more horizontal as she fainted with nerves collapsing like one of those goats straight into and obliterating a table just off stage.

"Hey Phil, while we call an ambulance for this lady can you start your set?"

I felt like a lemon being dried out by the sun, my skin was trying to almost crawl into my body.

It was go time.

See here is the thing I learned about confidence at this moment and something I have found to be true.

Confidence is the after-effect. It is the result of doing an action.

No one is confident before they try to ride a bike for the first time, but they get on, they fall off, they learn from falling and what not to do, they bump, bruise and scratch but eventually they learn they won't always fall. As a result of repeatedly doing the action, confidence arrives.

People wait around for the right feeling, or to feel confident before they do something.

The truth of life is, that confidence is in taking action.

When we are in action we are learning how to ride the bike. If we are looking at it waiting for confidence to come then we better bring a chair and some coffee because it'll take a long time.

Confidence = Action, Self doubt = Inaction.

When we sit in inaction we start to doubt. If I had not gotten on stage I would have sat there thinking about all the reasons not to go up, thought about what happened to the people before me, and thought about all the instances I wasn't funny in life. It is only human that our minds go there.

But look at what inaction would have brought me, enough self-doubt that I almost certainly would not have gotten up and would have crumpled.

Instead, I got up, I connected, I faced the fear and I didn't die, I didn't get booed off and I didn't collapse. I did pretty well!

Afterwards, I booked my next gig and you know what, I felt a little more confident.

Look at where you are stalling or feel stuck in life, and see where you can take action today. Make a commitment to taking action right now. Mel Robbins suggests the five-second rule where if you need to make a choice and not overthink then give yourself a five-second countdown and at the end of that countdown you must take action.

Action either creates excellent results or excellent lessons to learn from, either way, you are further down the road than the person sitting in overthinking.

FIGHTING WITH WHAT 'IS'

This has to be a universal feeling, we all fall into it at various points during our day.

You will know it when you start leaning on the term 'should'. Things should be this way, he should do this, I should do that.

When we start using the term should, we are wrong. Straight away we are wrong.

We are creating ways to argue with reality and what 'is'.

"My husband should be kinder to me" no he shouldn't because he isn't. No amount of shoulding will change what 'is'.

The more we use the word should, the further we get from dealing with reality. Should exclusively lives in your mind and is holding you from peace and calm.

Think about where in your life you are applying should and examine how the should is clouding you from what is.

RELATIONSHIPS

Boy, can they be tricky!

I don't think it is wild to say that is pretty universal.

I decided to address them late on in the book for a very purposeful reason.

Relationships are made infinitely more difficult and for me impossible if you have not done the inner work and know what you are showing up with.

We run into them or look for them as solutions to our problems. We look at someone else and say "ah-ha you there, you make me happy" then we are shocked when they are doing the same in some weird Mexican happiness stand-off. We are left hurt and disappointed because we lived relationships through our unspoken expectations.

I have run the gauntlet of hating myself so much that I dove into abusive relationships and toxic ones like an Olympic swimmer diving into a pool.

I didn't understand but I was seeking out people to prove my beliefs about myself right, which were ones of bile and hatred (see the chapter about ego) I wanted to be proven right.

When things got confusing and frustrating I started showing up as a terrible partner, being careless and absent-minded. Never looking inwards at my self-loathing and pain but always outwards. Blaming the world for my lack of self-love and understanding and as such hurting a lot of people along the way.

I believe until you know and understand yourself by doing deep inner work then relationships can be a minefield.

The most important relationship to work on is ALWAYS the one with yourself.

How much more appealing is the prospect of two people who fully understand their value, enjoy their lives and realise they are not solely dependent on the other person meeting up to enjoy life and love together sound?

THE RELATIONSHIP TRUTH

It is all about you!

Now before you go running to your partner saying "Yes! I knew it, Phil confirmed it's all about me me me!" I want to elaborate with a very sobering but incredibly powerful message.

You CAN NOT ever change what other people do, think about, say or feel.
This often angers people at first. The assumption is they have no control in their lives, but, that is the opposite of what is true, I am just showing where all of our control lies.

So we can not change others no matter how badly we want to, I had a client, Alice, out in Illinois in America. She was this amazing woman, CEO of her own business and thought so deeply about life, she just 'got it' all of our work together she picked up with ease, except when it came to her husband, session after session she would say how mad she was with him, how deeply she wanted him to be different. She thought he was lazy, uninterested, lost his passion and all sorts of things that were perfectly true.

But let's think about this with some powerful self-reflecting questions.

If someone angrily told you to change who you are would you?

If someone told you to be more interested could you? Or would you pretend for a bit and fall back into the same habits? Can you force something to be of interest?

Now someone can yell, nag or force someone to do something but how does that end? It brings resentment and anger. It breeds and festers and surfaces later down the line. It also reinforces an underlying belief that the other person is incapable of resolving that on their own. It lessens them.

The place the real power lies in our lives and relationships? It is with you.

We can not change how other people show up or react but we CAN decide how we show up, we can decide the meaning and story we will attach if any, and we can control how we react.

Imagine if you could go into an argument or discussion with your partner with that knowledge, that you do not have to react because you are seeing things as they are. You are just in control of yourself.

You can decide to show up with love and kindness instead of harsh angry reactions.

This doesn't mean allowing everything another person wants to do or making them right.

What it means is that you can calmly tell them what you stand for and how it affects you.

The awesome power of releasing the idea that you can change someone can be something special.

You have only one thing to focus on, one thing you can control so all of your energy should go there, right? It doesn't have to be a million tiny pieces in a million directions, but rather it's giving your all for you.

I remember when my beautiful and amazingly patient wife and I first moved in together. She was so much more organised than I was, I was relaxed by nature. My Grandparents would always say I was so laid back I may as well be horizontal! My wife did not operate from that space.

I would get so frustrated at her intense need for things to be organised and on time. I would get so angry that she couldn't see things my way. Surely I have shown her how cool being laid back can be right? Look how cool I am!

This was a fiery confrontation that I feel lasted months if not years. Two people wanting the other to fold and bow to the others way of thinking.

The real shift in our relationship came when we started looking at ourselves instead of each other. I decided to look at how I could bring my best self to each moment of the relationship and when I asked that question and thought about it, the best 'me' doesn't show up lazy (Which I was totally doing) but the best me acts from love and kindness. By doing this it created space for my wife to explore doing the same and we created a way of working that was built upon love and respect and not our ego.

Stop and ask yourself, what would the best version of me BE in this situation.
BE that.

THE MYTH OF THE 50/50 RELATIONSHIP

There is a myth peddled around the world today that relationships are 50/50 and that is both damaging and untrue.

Relationships, the good ones, are 100/100.

You see if relationships are 50/50 then you only have to bring half and there is room for the numbers to get skewed. You may only bring 20% or 80% and the other brings more or less. It is a sliding scale of arguments and conflict.

Instead, consider that every relationship is 100/100. It requires that you both bring 100% of yourself regardless of what the other person is bringing. You have no control over what they bring! So stop thinking about it. Your goal as of right now is to start bringing 100% of you to every relationship, why would you bring less? It is your responsibility as an owner of life to bring this. If you bring it, the other person feels permission for them to bring the same.

Consider for yourself now, are you bringing your 100%?

SELF LOVE

I wish there was a better term than self-love I do. If you have never experienced having a group of friends with the emotional maturity of teenagers then you do not know the horror of having to say self-love constantly and being met with sniggering.

Some say self-care, but I think that is too weak for what I am talking about, self-care is vital but I am talking about holding a deep place of love for yourself and comparing it to a facemask, beer and cheese (my wife's favourite combo) doesn't seem right.

When I started coaching I used to get frustrated that things were moving so slowly. I felt like I had this amazing gift but so few to give it to. I started using marketing gurus, advertisements, and tactics and quite frankly met a lot of gross and slimy types. I was miserable.

I wanted to grow my business authentically and from the heart. So one day I was at one of my lowest points, I was in a deep depression, and I wanted to quit the business and just go back to doing 9 to 5. I thought I will attend one more session with my coach then I am done.

During this session my first transformation happened, I did the whole session just focused on me, not my business, not my coaching, me and my treasure chest of crap. I worked hard and we went deep into my thoughts and beliefs.

I started showing up differently. People got to see this version of me and everything in my life started opening up.

The number one truth in life is you are loved, if you choose to look at your relationship with yourself and work on it your whole world will change!

Here is an exercise I learned from a wonderful coach allied Amber Krys that helps you understand self-love -

Imagine someone or something you love, it can be a child/newborn or a dog, or a partner just something you know you unconditionally love.

You will know the thing to pick because at someone point you will have had those moments, where you are staring into their eyes, they are looking back at you and the thoughts of the world don't come in. You are not thinking about work, planning or how you look. You are just in that moment.

That is how self-love can feel. That is the eyes to look at yourself through. With love, empathy and forgiveness.

When I talk about self-love, that is the feeling I mean.

THE AUTHENTIC VS THE CONDITIONED SELF

When we are born we are what is known as the 'Authentic self'. Babies do not have any judgements, they do not question if they are worthy of receiving love and when they look into your eyes you feel it, that unconditional deep love. This is who you are, it is who we all are. We are beings who are authentically self-loving.

As we grow older we attach ourselves and our meaning to stories to help us fit in and survive, stories like 'I am too fat' 'I am too skinny' 'I am too much for people' 'I need to be perfect' 'I should be less lazy and a whole host of negative messages we smash ourselves with every day.

This is what makes up what we call a personality or our conditioned self. It is false, the personality is just a set of stories and lies we have told or been told that we have collected and made into a way of being.

Do you know a sure-fire way to show the personality is false? Take someone who has a personality of being a grumpy, angry and tough old bloke, someone who works late hours in a factory and never shows emotion and then hand him his baby grandchild. Watch his personality melt away as he connects to what is universally within all of us, that deep love for our authentic self. He isn't seeing the anger and pain in his life, the judgements he makes about himself, all he sees is the love given and love received.

The personality we create can also be referred to as our ego, which Freud suggested is controlled by our superego, which is kind of a self-made idea of ourselves as gods in our universe.

Our society is sadly built to make us forget that we are all loveable, there are enough messages about our bodies alone on how we should look and act to keep us in a state of shame for our whole life.

However, love is there for you. It is in you and it IS you. Confused? Excited? GOOD! I want to invite you to approach all of this with an open mind and heart and you will see what I mean.

Exercise -THE SELF LOVE MONOLOGUE

- *Pair up -> Person A & Person B*
- *A it is your task to talk about self-love for ten minutes, no less.*
- *B you are not allowed to make ANY comments during this.*
- *Ok B now it is your turn to talk about self-love, again for ten minutes.*
- *This exercise can be done on your own using a device to record and watch it back.*

This exercise can feel extremely difficult, a lot of people say that ten minutes is too long, and some say it is something they have never really thought about. The goal is to get you to start a deep inquiry into what self-love is for you.

Try also writing down your answer to the following "To me, self-love is….."

Self-love is deeper than any kind of verb - It is the very fabric of who you are. " a loving attitude from which positive actions arise that benefit you and others"

SELF-LOVE VS SELF CARE

When I have done this exercise and asked people the question of what self-love is, often they respond with 'taking time for a hot bath' or 'a night with the TV' or 'wearing a facemask' and while this certainly can be part of it, I would usually class these acts as 'Self-care.

Self-love, as we will be referring to it here, is the re-connecting and becoming aligned to our authentic self, realising powerful truths that you are worthy and you are valuable.

Being human is messy, we all make mistakes and mess up pretty constantly, but if we can create a purpose and an awareness of self-love then we can gradually get closer to a place of alignment.

Why do we lose our authentic selves?

We never lose it, we only ever forget. The society we exist within is rigged to make us forget. We are bombarded with messages that you can only feel proud of if you look like this, you will only be worthy if you make this much money, and your talent is worthless because you are not as famous as whoever. This creates and influences everyone, who passes this on and it spreads like wildfire.

Sounds scary! What do I do when I forget?

The times when we feel that we have forgotten, are in moments of real struggle and lack of fulfilment. When this happens we have usually bought into our own stories, that we are someone who can't cope, that we are alone, that we are not worthy of being loved.

When we do the work and focus on our relationship with ourselves we can create an awareness and through that awareness, a little crack of light of self-appreciation can start to shine in.

The following are 4 key principles of what self-love is.

1- SELF-LOVE IS WHO YOU ARE BEING

The learned self finds it so difficult to answer big questions like "who am I?" or "what do I want?" It also hates to describe itself in job interviews and write about itself on dating profiles. It has no awareness because it is made entirely of second-hand knowledge and our judgements.

Self-love is a connection to our unconditioned self - far beyond the body, the masks, the outer shell, our ego and our personality. You can start to let yourself feel who you truly are.

2- SELF-LOVE IS KNOWING YOU ARE MADE OF LOVE

Self-love, although two separate words are NOT two separate things. Love is who you are, let me be clear I am not saying that you have love inside of you, I am saying that you ARE love itself. It is the original energy of your authentic self.

Our personalities don't know how to love, they are not made for it, they try but they are made from judgments and stories.

This is why when you or someone else relaxes and detaches from their personality telling them all the judgements that people may be passing out or that it is passing out itself, that person is seen as much more attractive and fun, they are closer to their authentic self and therefore love.

3 - SELF-LOVE IS HOW YOU REALLY FEEL ABOUT YOURSELF

Self-love is often thought of as being difficult, fragile or even hard work.

So many of the population (and I was in this space for so many years) are avoiding spending quiet concentrated time with myself to avoid the endless hoard of harsh self-judgement. When we are in this place we are being identified solely as our personality and can't imagine a version of doing this without the attack.

The truth, the real truth is that your Authentic Self, which is love, loves you and does so very much.

The Irish priest and poet John O'Donohue wrote " Your soul longs to draw you in to love for yourself. When you enter your soul's affection, the torment in your life ceases"
This quote is beautiful and it may be one you want to read a few times over.

So while our personality is always looking outward for love, what we have to realise is that our Authentic self IS love.

There is not some journey out there to get to love, but rather it is with all of right now.

Now is time to finally stop, breathe and relax, give your personality some time off and allow yourself to feel how much your Authentic Self accepts, affirms and cherishes you in every moment.

4 - SELF-LOVE IS A COMMITMENT

Self-love can be a vow we make when we enter the world to always remember our authentic self and to try and not get lost in appearances.

Although we start as children we grow up to become a bunch of separate egos, then as we grow older we start to realise that there is something more to us than our body, image and our stories. It is almost an unspoken, indescribable sensation that hits you.

I suggest that we never reach ourselves, we have always been Self and we are just remembering. That is our promise, to remember this Self from now on.

Self-love is natural and not shameful and it is the key to being you. We live in a world where the term loving yourself is a replacement for narcissism. Deep down we know self-love is not this, it is caring, and forgiving and it is how you honour yourself, how you start to see your secret beauty and awesomeness.

The more and more you accept my invitation to love yourself the more you will get what being yourself means, it empowers you!

From here I want you to make a promise to yourself that "I will NOT forget who I am" and "I will NOT abandon myself". Each time you go to belittle yourself in some way, call upon your true authentic self to help you choose self-love instead.

When we are in a relationship realise to love somebody is a commitment saying "I won't forget who you are, I won't abandon you and together we will remember what is real"

CLOSING THOUGHTS

I wanted to thank you for reading my book.

Really and truthfully from the bottom of my heart, it means the world to me.

I have no desire on becoming a best-selling author, but the fact this book made it into the hands of someone who is on a journey of self-exploration makes me excited for what you will create and who you decide to show up as in the future.

I would rather this book fell into the hands of ten people who would value the message and use it than thousands of people just looking for something to read.

I would ask you to do three things from here.

Firstly make a personal inner commitment to yourself, to create a self that is magnificent and a joy in the world. Never stop working on this and send me your journey. (details below)

Secondly, if you enjoyed this book and think you know someone who would benefit from it, please share it and pass it out to family members or members of the public you think could use it.

Finally.

Every single day.

Slow down, show up and live.

Cheers
Phil

If you would like to leave feedback on the book, discuss the ideas or want to explore hiring me as your coach please contact me via the following channels.

Website: www.pmalifecoaching.com
Email: thepmacoaching@gmail.com

A PAGE OF GRATITUDE

I give deep thanks and love to all of the following people, you have shaped my life and my being forever on my journey of creating SSL. Every single one of you has brought something unique to my life and has helped me grow and deepen my experience in life. I thank you all from the bottom of my heart.

My parents, Gran- You have stood by me when others wouldn't have. You have guided me and helped me beyond what anyone would expect. I love you all and thank you.

My friends - You helped me create and go out on my own, you read my drafts, and you kept me grounded. Kris and Rob, you helped me start my crazy idea for a business and helped me when I needed it most. Thank you, my brothers.

My family-in-law- Showed me love and support regardless of the insane decisions I was making.

Becky Smiles - Your love and passion for your family is second to none.

Jessica Rich - After all these years, if we speak every week for the rest of time it will not be enough. You are a real light and a joy in the world

Paula & Mike Ryan - Two souls who taught me as much about myself as anyone. A family filled with heart.

Samantha McGee - Keep being the badass the world needs. You are an incredible force.

Rasha Arubas - With a heart as big as yours you will always succeed.

Martin Milner - Being all that you are, life is just beginning for you.

Tanner Fanello - An incredible father, son and husband. It came into existence when you spoke it, my friend.

Paul Terry - The king. Need I say more my friend.

Matthew Bollands - Watching you take our sessions into everyday life and succeed has been one of the greatest joys of my entire professional career.

Komal Samuel - When you share your love, I just know it will be life-changing for everyone.

Anna Race - Being you is always good enough. It is even more.

Hannah Fernando - Whatever you decide to do, I know you will do it better than anyone.
Tahira Batool - When you find yourself, the world will be yours as will its love.
Katherine Curry - The Smee to my Hook
Josie Garner - Your sureness of self and the power you hold stunned me every time.
Adam Slobodzian - My brother, you helped me start my journey. For life.

I also want to give a special thank you to Jude Daunt for being my gateway into the world of coaching and being a constant support, mentor and friend.

And finally to David Wilkinson, my friend, my guide, my coach and my brother. You have inspired me and taught me more than I thought I would ever achieve. You have helped me to create my life of magnificence. Long may you continue to do so.

Printed in Great Britain
by Amazon